HARD

William Giancursio

H

H A R D

ISBN 978-0-6152-4469-3

H A R D

We are a culture of men obsessed with being hard. We work hard, play hard and want our bodies, especially certain parts, to be hard all the time. Life is hard. Often the amount of satisfaction we derive from accomplishment is comparable to the degree of difficulty we overcome in our quest to obtain our goals. This book was hard but well worth the effort.

It is also hard to describe the exhilarating feeling that comes from building the sets and props. The many long hours spent staging and photographing them seem to vanish as I immerse myself into a world of make-believe. Most of the photos were shot in my studio. At first I tried to set up outdoors in a parking lot so as to capture the view through the windows. I spend an entire summer waiting for the precise day when the wind was calm and the temperature was just right. On several occasions I attempted to set up the entire gym only to have the wind blow it down. The intense sun was always a factor in lighting the set. The heat would often cause the action figures to "wilt" and fall over, just as I was about to snap a photo.

At last the perfect day arrived. I eagerly and carefully packed my van and drove out to the location. I spent most of the day capturing some remarkable shots. When I returned home that evening, exhausted, I discovered that I had forgotten to load the memory chip into the camera. The 300 or so photos I had taken were nowhere to be found, but I had learned a valuable lesson the hard way.

HARD is my second photo book. It is another in an ongoing series of gay-play books that represent my visual journal of gay culture. Once again I take a lyrical look at who we are, what we do, and some of our aspirations. Our Gay Wedding Day is the first in the series. Although amusing on many levels, it confronts the viewer with same-sex marriage equality. HARD, on the other hand, takes a closer look at a day at a gay gym.

The gym and all of its many assorted pieces took close to a year to construct. Elements like the exercise equipment, the lockers and their tiny locks were a real challenge to build as were the urinals and other parts of the men's room and juice bar. I wanted the scale to be accurate and convincing to the eye of the camera. It took another six months to shoot and sort through more than 2500 digital photographs that I have taken with my Canon Rebel XT.

I had a general idea of my objective but I didn't follow a storyboard or rigid narrative. Some of the photos appear to be sequential, while others are just random shots that I liked and wanted to include. The concept of the photographer and his dog being photographed while photographing the others was an afterthought, one that I used to help weave the storyline together.

I must admit to naming several of the "men" and even giving them a profile. Blake and Josh are two perfect men who meet at the gym and develop this insane attraction for each other. James and Seth are the more established gay couple. They drive the 1957 turquoise Chevy. The third couple, Karl and Stephen, are somewhat closeted. Karl, a firefighter, is the older of the two. Stephen is his boy-toy. Mike is a personal trainer and the bartender at Juice. Kyle runs the front desk while Peter, the guy in the red v-neck t-shirt and cargo shorts, is mostly a pasty looking voyeur who rarely exercises yet seems to lurk everywhere. I am Bill the photographer and that's my dog Arrow. We hope you enjoy our book.

Stay HARD.

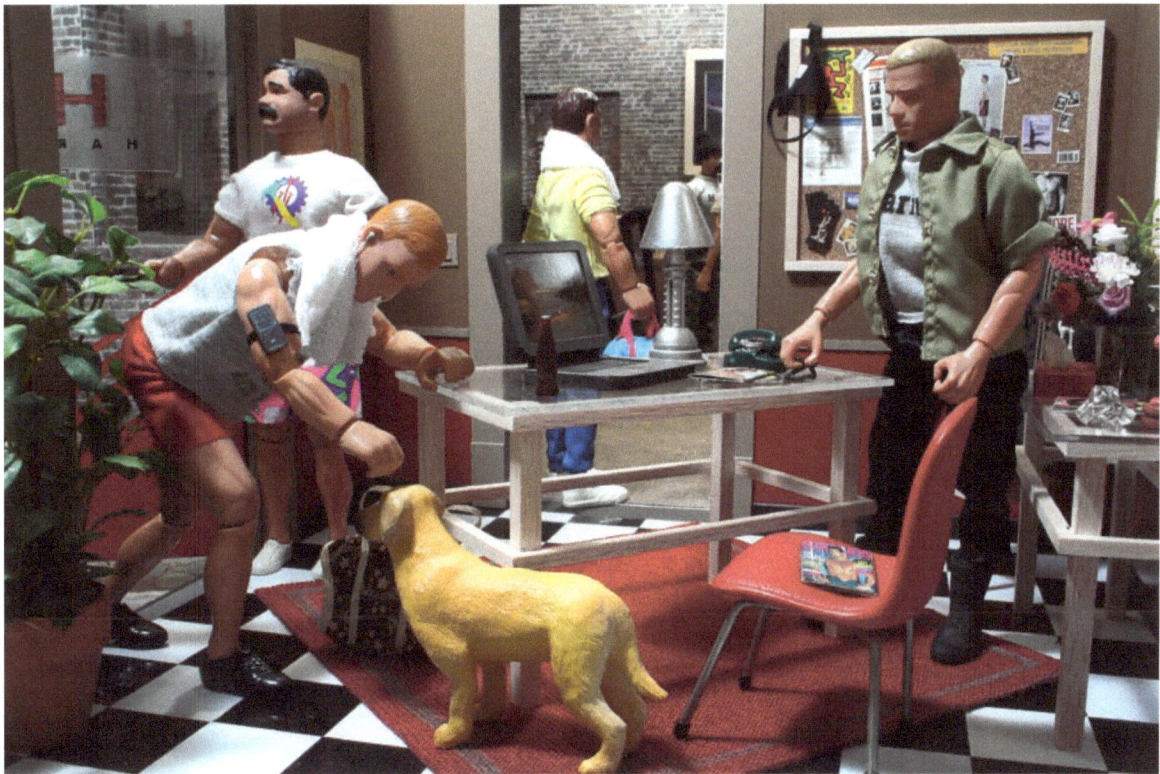

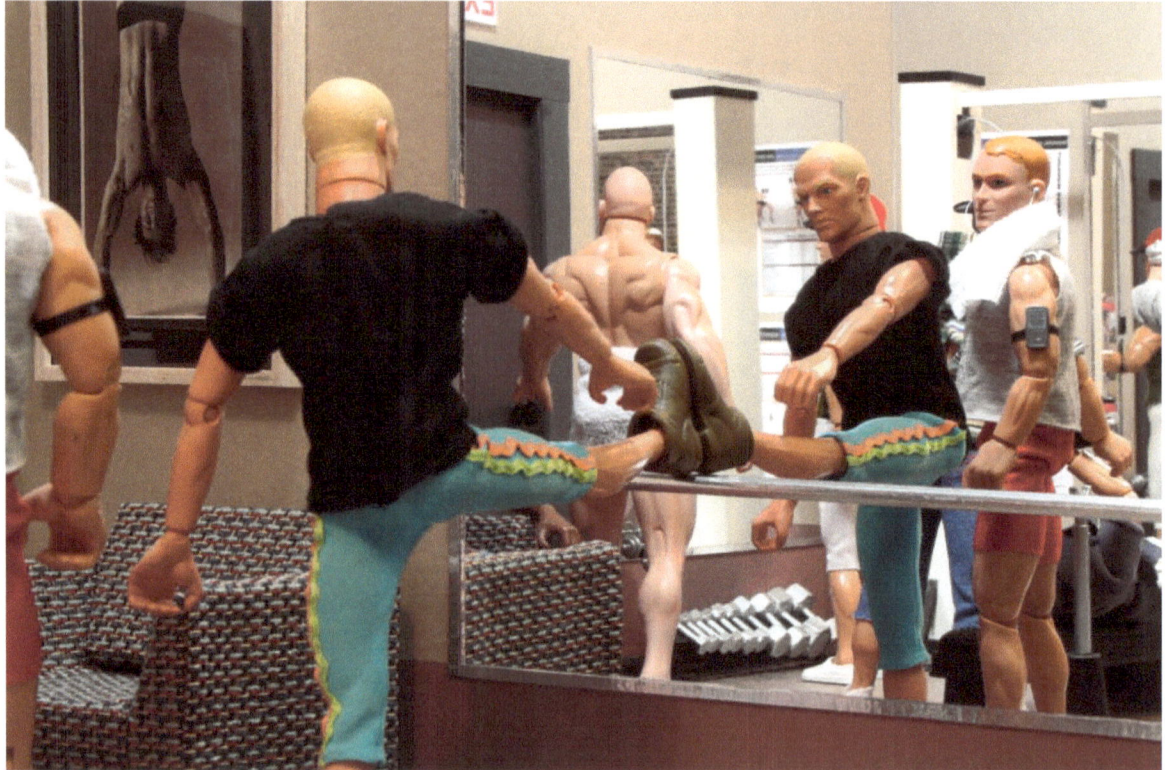

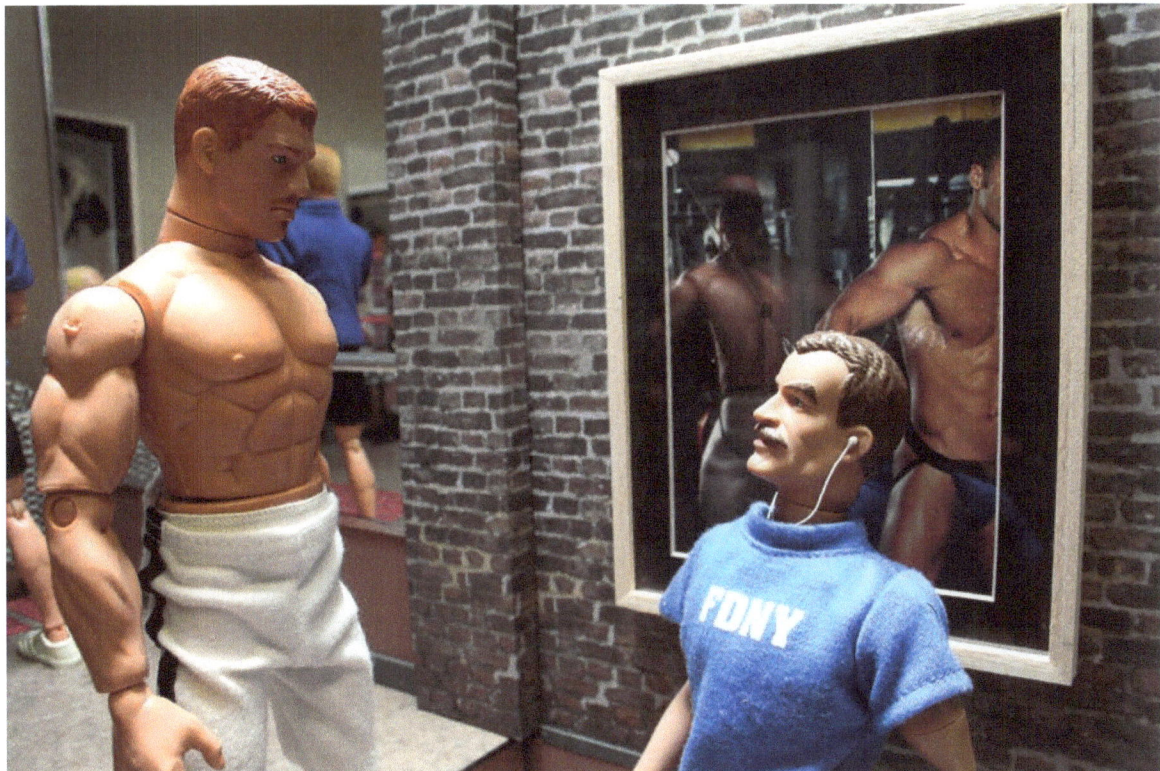

43

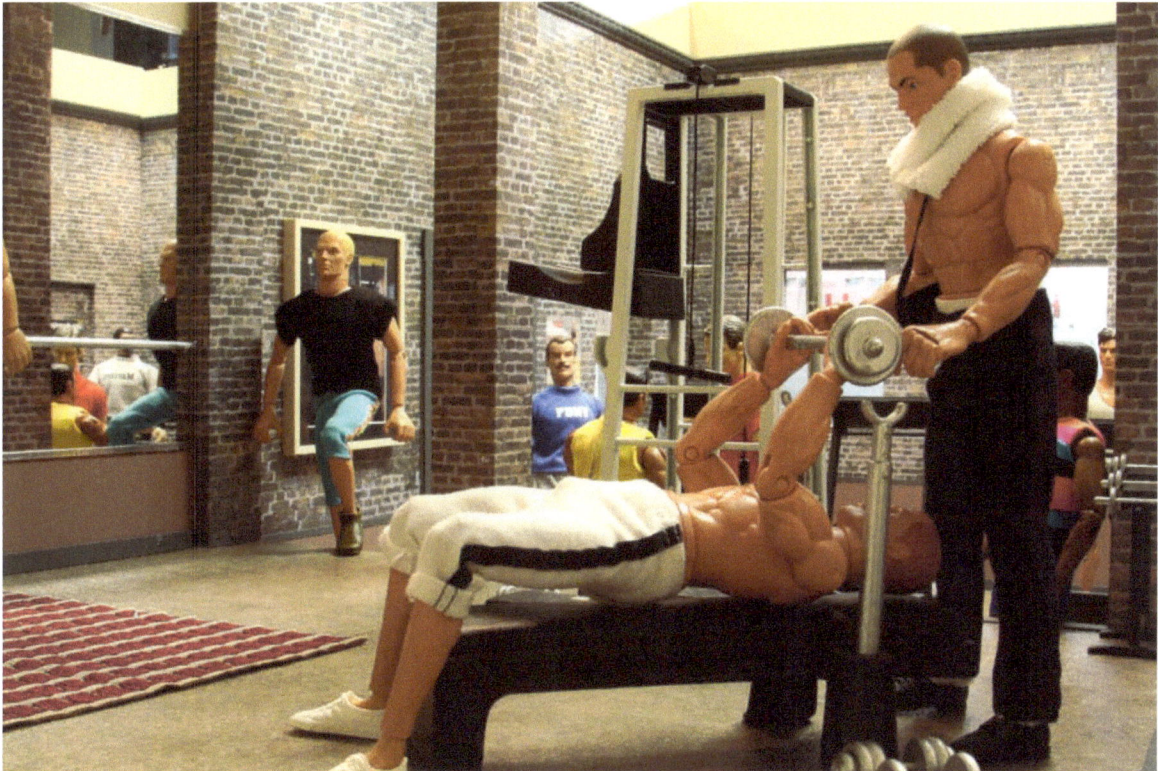

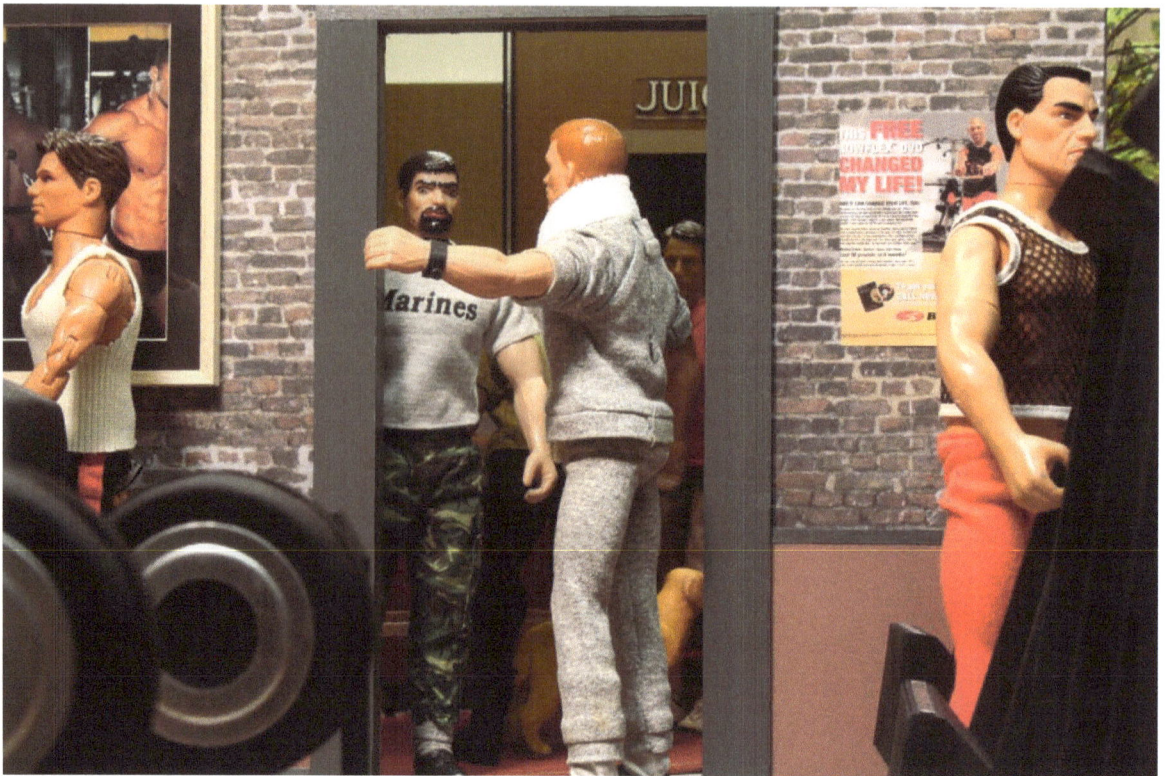

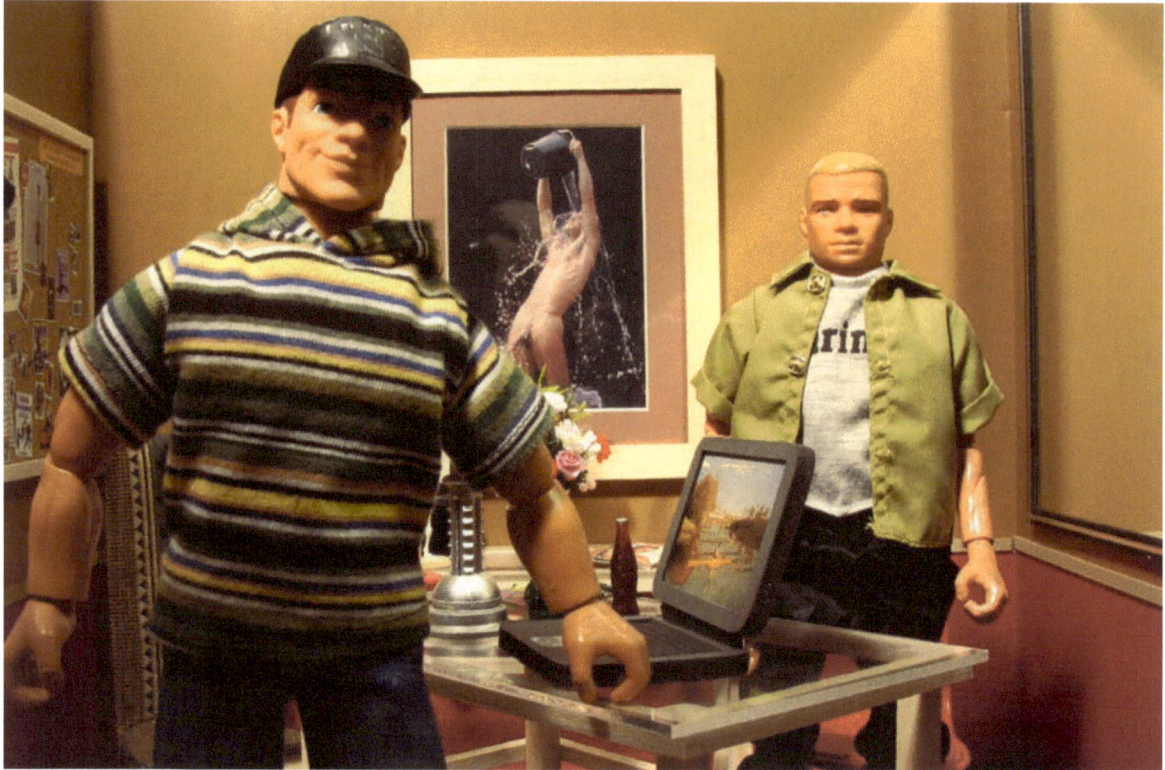

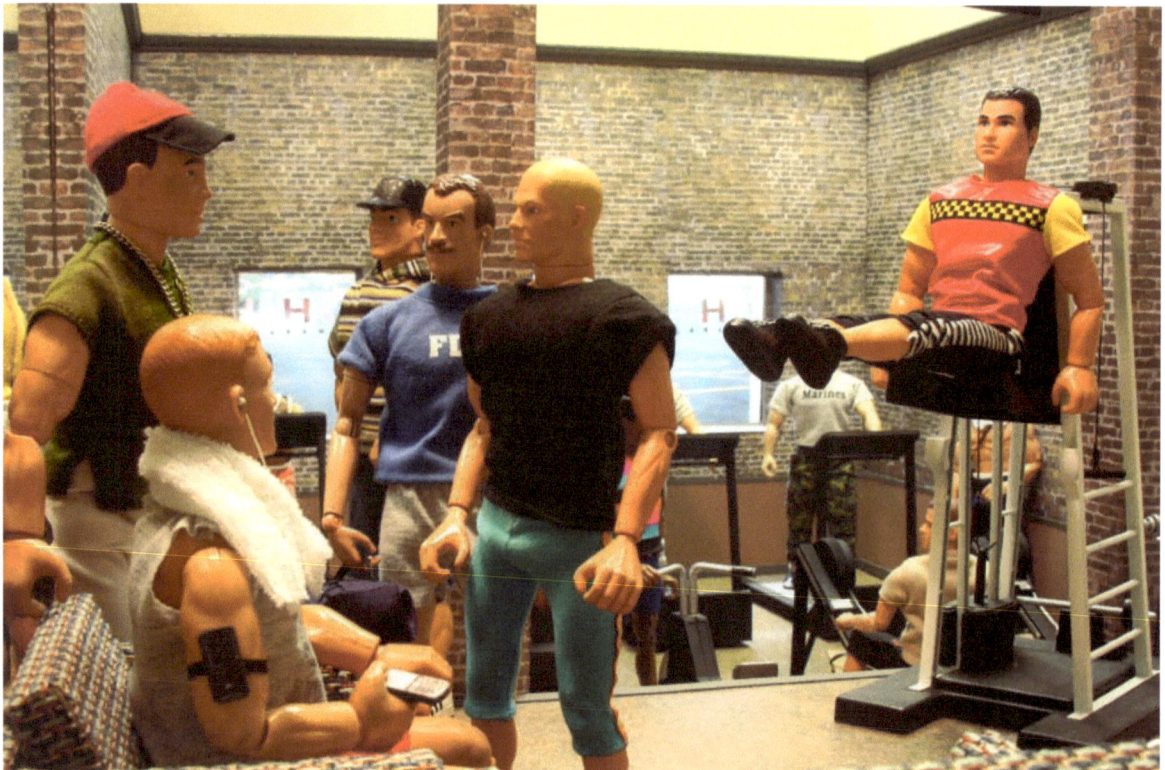

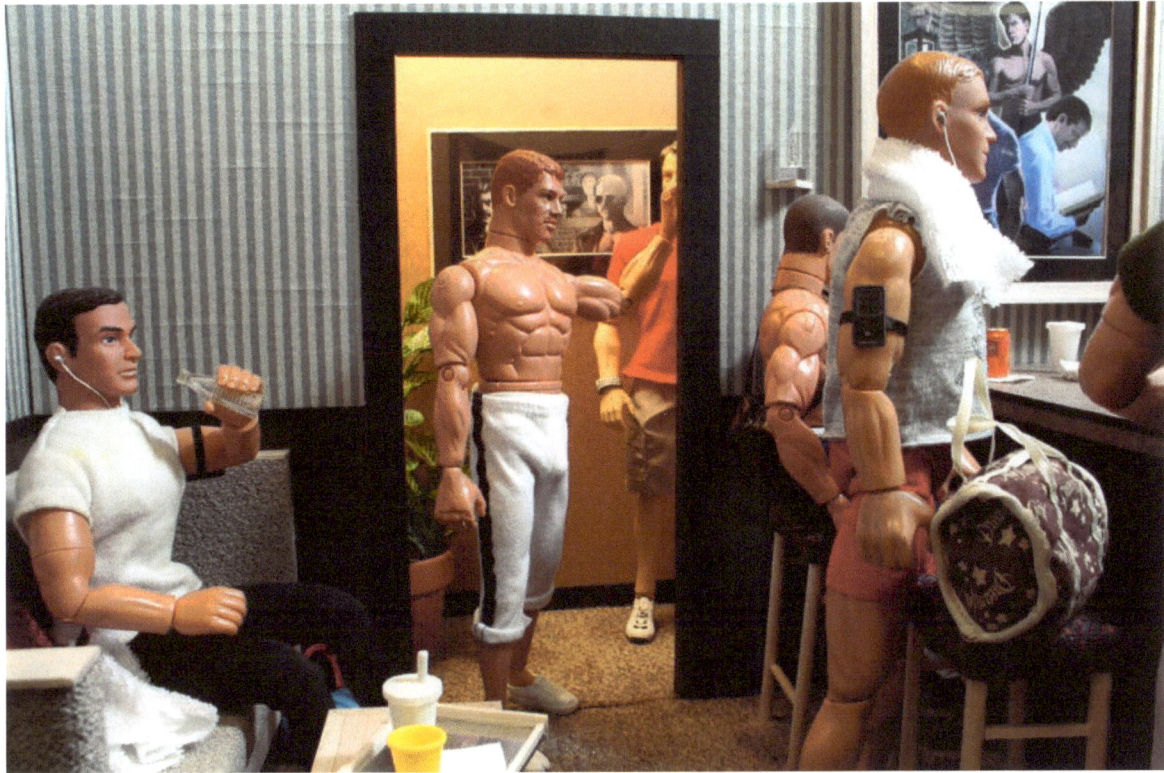

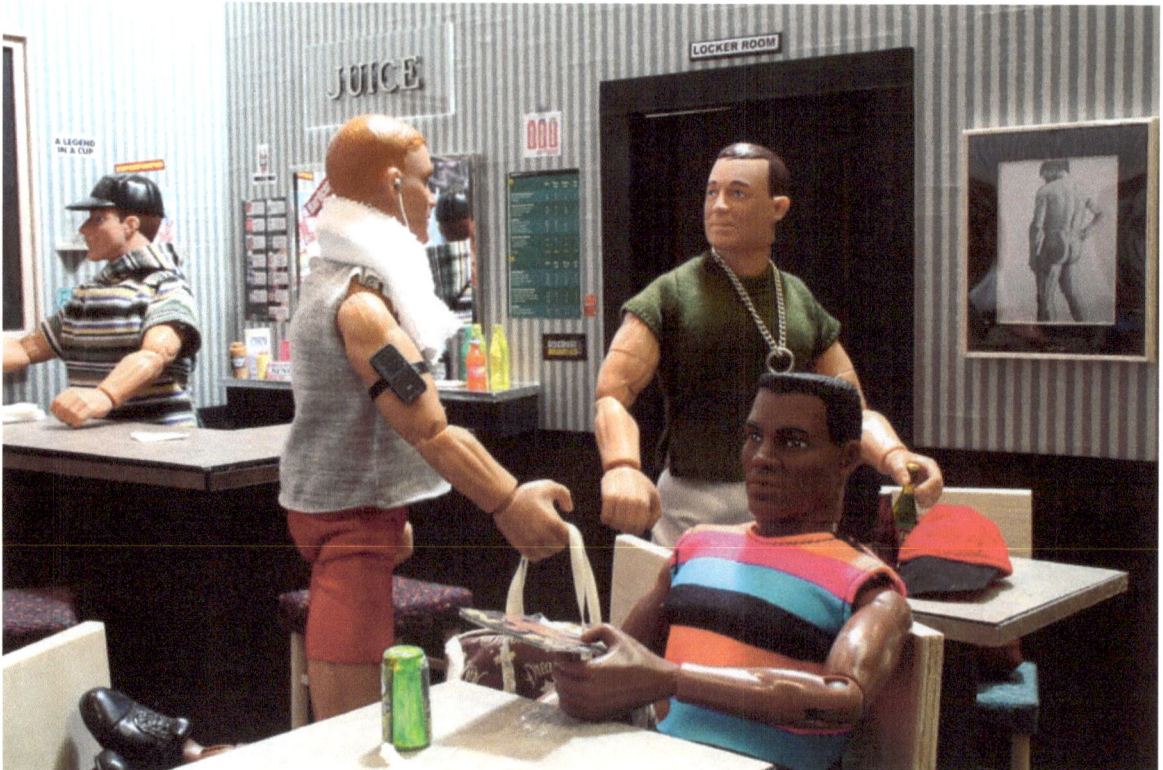

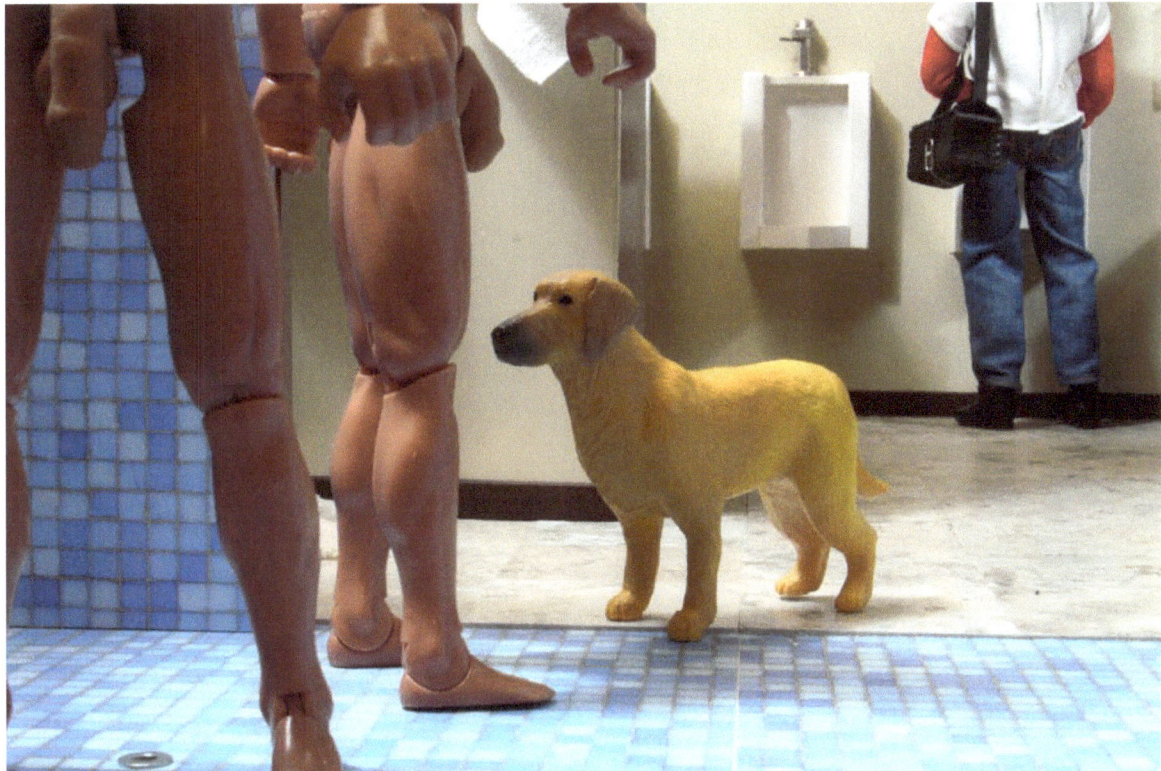

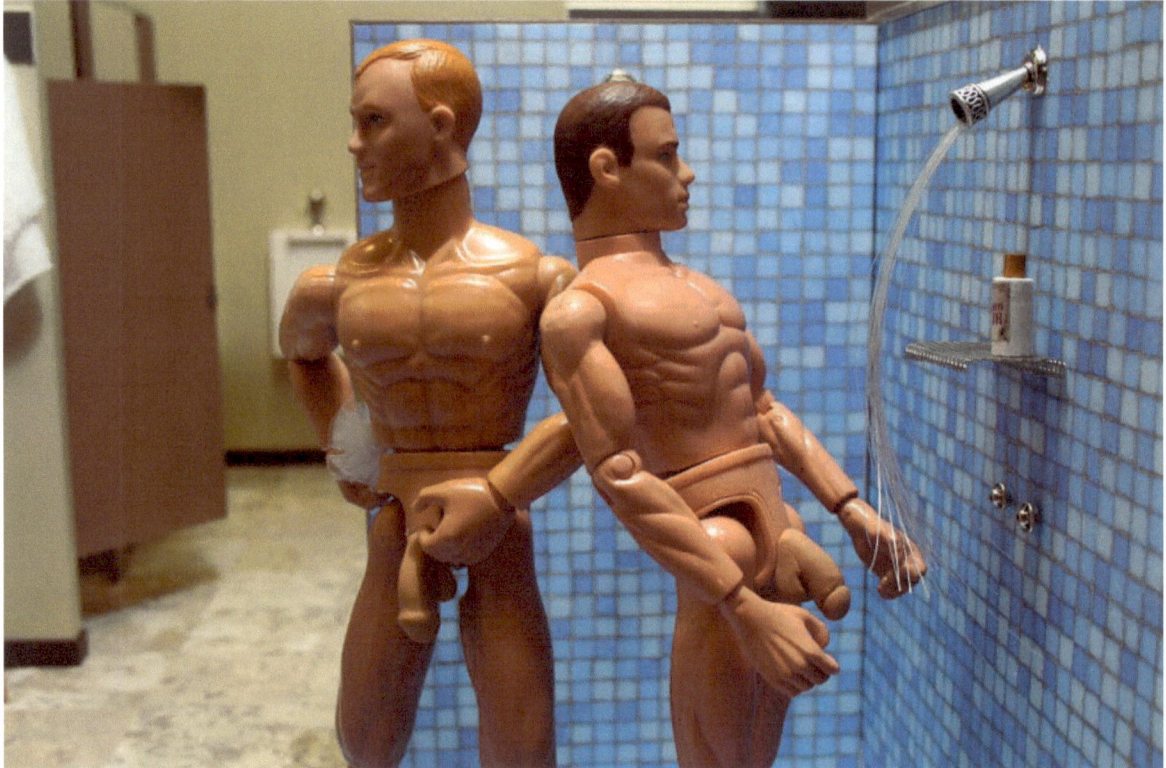

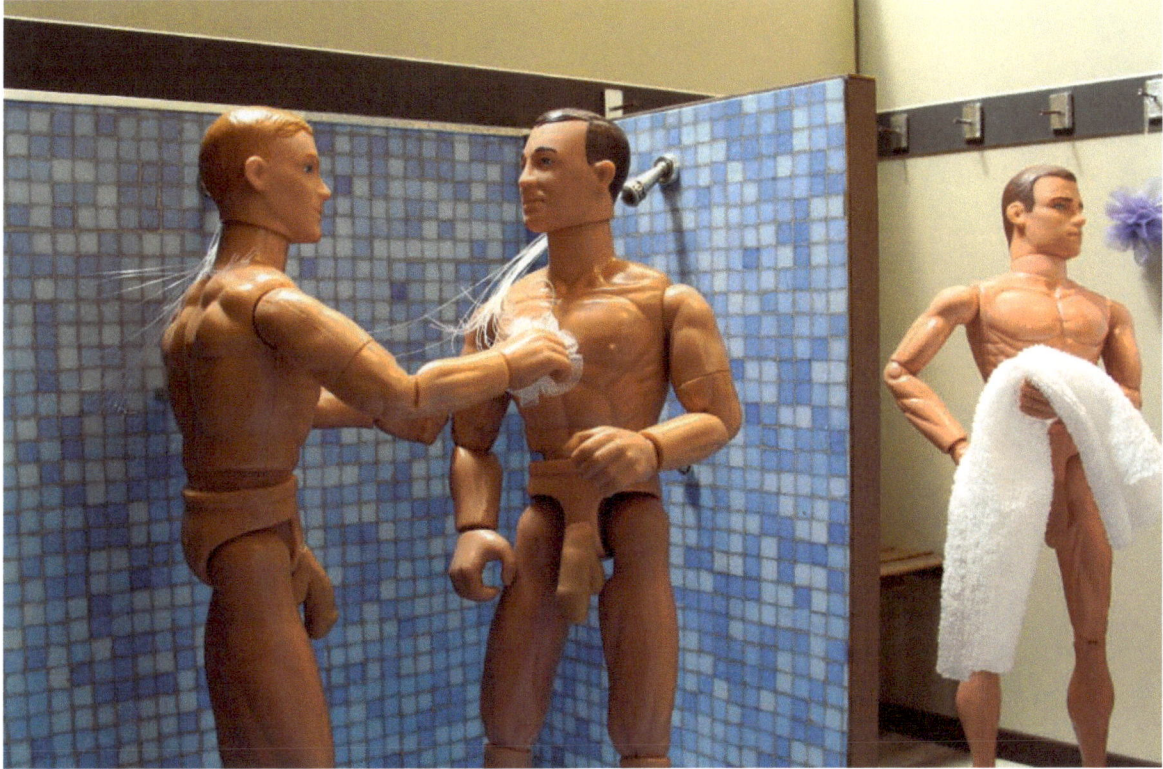

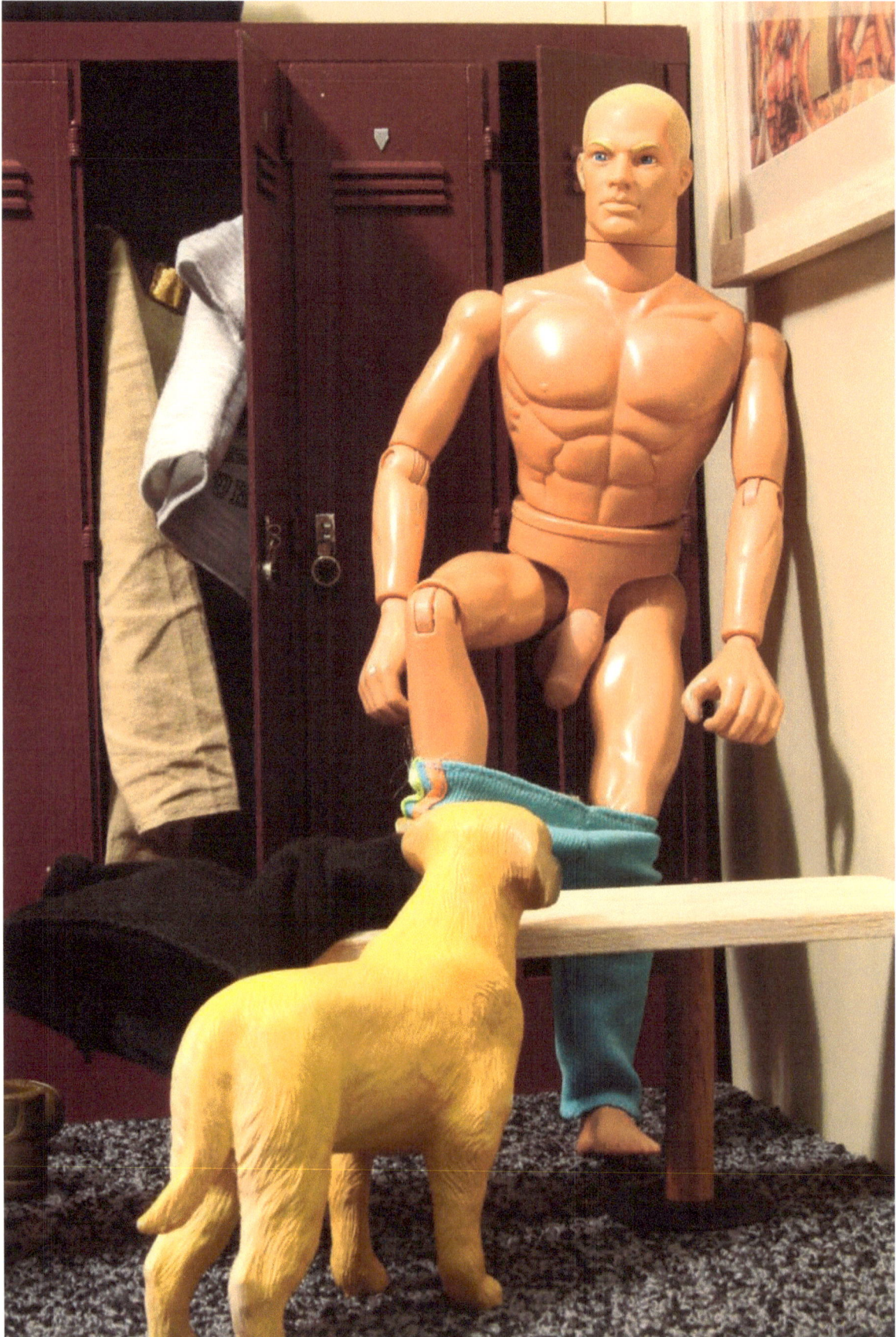

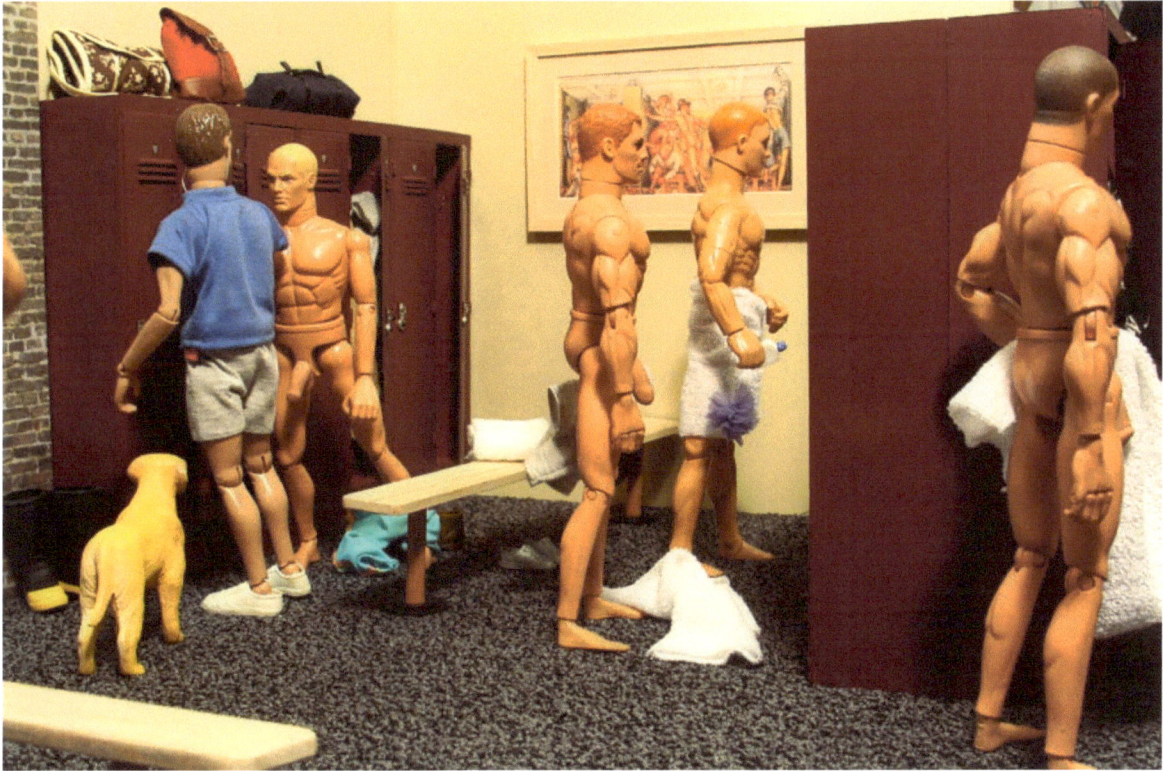

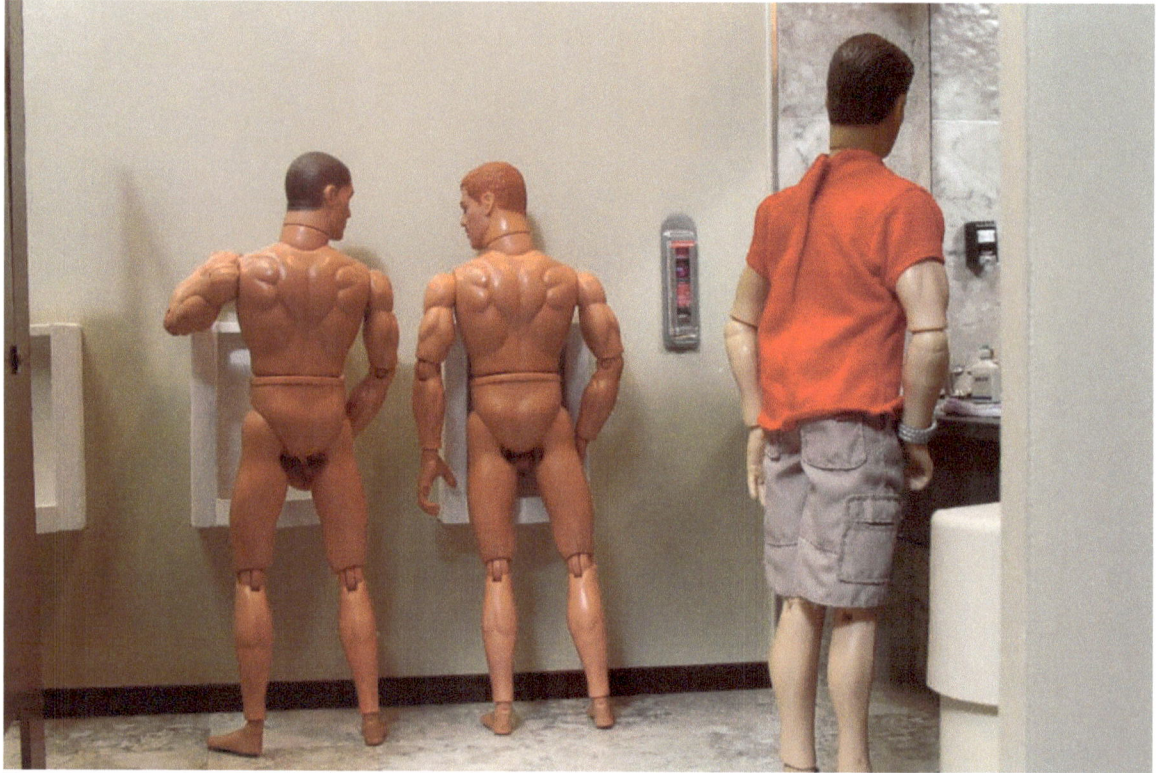

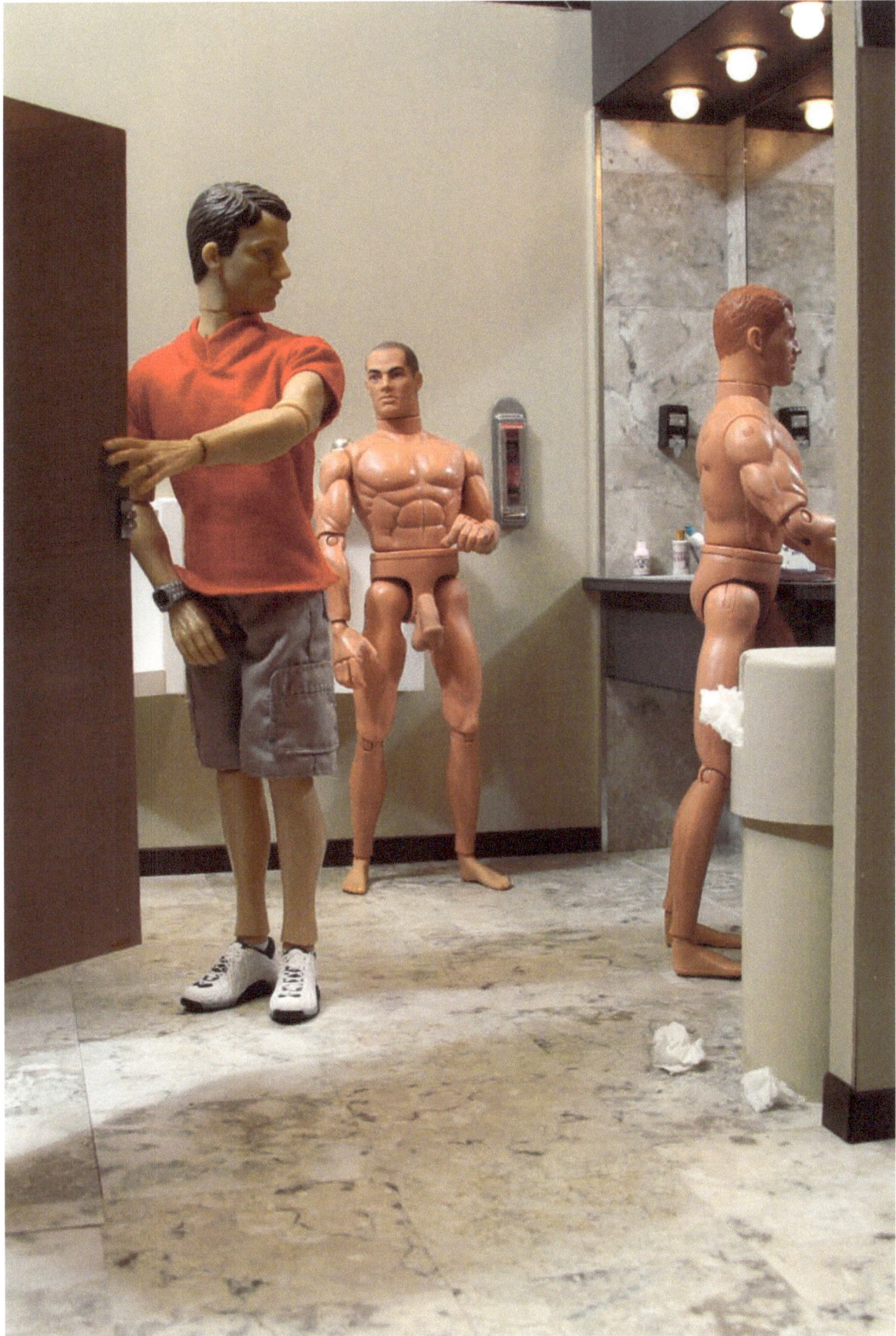

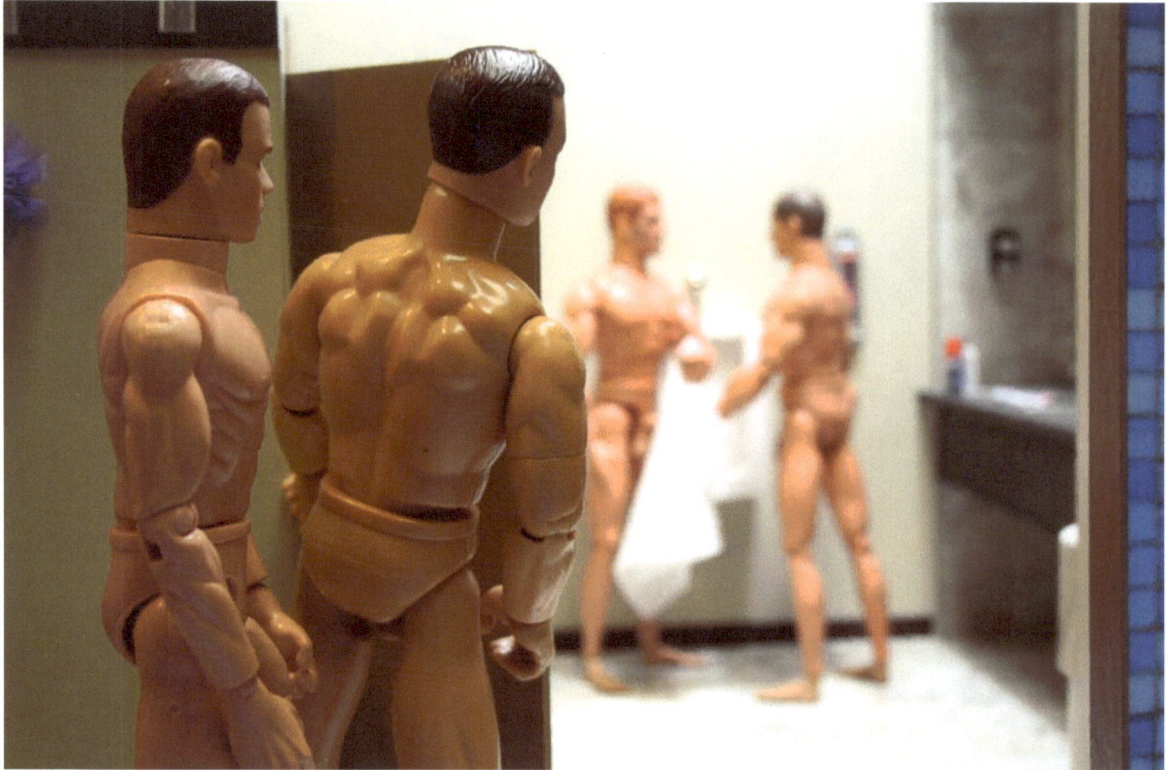

www.ingramcontent.com/pod-product-compliance
Lightning Source LLC
Chambersburg PA
CBHW041421290326
41932CB00042B/37

* 9 7 8 0 6 1 5 2 4 4 6 9 3 *